"I love to photograph nature's beauties.
Senses, I discover that the camera lens ᵢ

same things. They uncover connections between me and the earth. As I
frame what delights me—mossy waterfalls, bluebonnet fields, icy creeks,
drifting fog—the everyday metamorphoses into the extraordinary. I feel
like it is possible to hear colours and taste shapes. I simply accept this
delightful sensory symphony, and focus the camera on such quiet
wonders."   ~ Linda Garrett

❀ ❀ ❀

"Sometimes people come along with a deep understanding of something,
which in itself is a great gift. But when they also possess an ability to
communicate that understanding to others in a way that deeply heals and
connects, you have a special kind of magic. Sami Aaron possesses that in
her connection to the beauty and deep healing potential of the natural world
and its relation to our lives. Experiencing her wisdom is a delight."

~ Elaina Cochran, ElatedEarth

❀ ❀ ❀

"Connecting to our larger community of humanity through nature becomes
increasingly more relevant in today's world. The Nature Process empowers
you to feel the connection and act at whatever level is appropriate for
you...without judgment. While I have always felt a comfort in nature, the
Nature Process retreat with Sami and this workbook opened me to a new
level of joy and awareness."   ~ Dena Klein

❀ ❀ ❀

"My love and appreciation of nature - its ability to heal, nurture and guide
- has been greatly enhanced by Sami's generous and passionate efforts on
behalf of The Nature Process. She has encouraged a more profound
understanding of the integral force of nature on our well-being as a species.
With love and gratitude."   ~ Susan Hangauer

EXPERIENCE YOUR 54 SENSES

Sept. 2017

For Vivvan—
   May your senses guide
you to a deeper understanding
of ego. and all that entails.
   So grateful for those deep
conversations we have.
              Love + light—
                  Sami

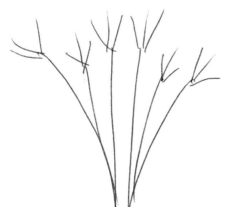

EXPERIENCE YOUR
YOUR
54 SENSES

A Companion Workbook for

The Nature Process®

Sami Aaron

Contents

Forward

When I first published the book *54 Days 54 Senses* it was written primarily for a corporate environment. Sami came to me and said that she could see how this could be expanded to reach a wider audience. I told her if she was attracted to doing something to go ahead!

What Sami's created with her book is a series of exercises that go far deeper into the 54 senses than in the first book and allow people anywhere to explore them and deepen their understanding of their 54 senses.

After seeing what Sami's created with this workbook I knew that we needed to discontinue the first book and replace it with Sami's.

The 54 senses are a key part of The Nature Process and the more you are able to explore your senses, the deeper you are able to connect to nature and experience the many benefits of doing so.

Sami's workbook offers a valuable contribution to those who have already experienced the power of The Nature Process as well as to those who aren't yet familiar with it.

It offers an easy and simple way to start being more mindful of nature today.

Tabitha Jayne, BSc, MSc, MBPsS, CPC
Creator: The Nature Process®

Introduction

The 54 Senses are an integral part of The Nature Process, a simple way of deepening your connection to nature by being in the body and experiencing nature through the senses so that you can reduce stress and improve your well-being.

Developed by Scottish applied psychologist Tabitha Jayne in 2014, The Nature Process is based on research that shows that spending time in nature improves your psychological, physical, social, and spiritual well-being.

Now, you may be thinking "54 Senses? What??? I thought I just had five!!"

Technically, yes, you have your senses of sight, sound, smell, taste, and touch. But these are just gateways to a deeper connection with the world around you. This workbook offers simple exercises that will teach you how to open and expand each of these familiar senses.

When you tune into this expansive state you'll notice that your "monkey-mind" settles, and you begin to think more clearly. You'll feel more at ease in your surroundings and more in touch with your body. These benefits are part of every meditation and mindfulness practice: tools that quiet the mind and nurture the heart.

A Google search on the word "meditation" results in more than 150 million hits. Humans are obviously on a mission to find ease and stillness in the midst of everyday stress and in times of grief, pain, and anxiety!

3

Here's An Example

Let me give you an example of someone with an expanded awareness of his senses.

Did you see the 1985 movie, *Crocodile Dundee*? It's the story of bushman Mick Dundee, from Walkabout Creek in the Australian outback, who has remarkable powers of observation about nature.

- With just a quick glance at the sun, he knows the exact time of day.
- With an intense stare and some hand gestures, he hypnotizes a water buffalo in Australia and two ferocious rotweillers in New York City. Like blobs of honey, they melt at his feet.
- He spears a giant fish with ease and snatches a poisonous snake with his bare hands – mid-sentence and in the dark, no less!

Do you think you could ever be as in touch with all your senses as Crocodile Dundee was? Was he born with more skills than you were? Believe it or not, you have all the same senses Mick does! It's just that you've never been taught to use them – or you've been taught to shut them off or ignore them.

Here's a quick exercise to help you get a feel for what this workbook will teach you:

As you read the next few pages, slow down and tap into your familiar senses of touch, sight, and sound.

- Notice the feel of the page against your fingertips as you read.
- Do you have a sense of the weight of the book?
- Take note of the movement of your hands and the tug of gravity that draws your arms toward the earth.
- Soften your gaze and notice the text and patterns you see on the page.
- What do you notice about form and design?

- What can you see in your peripheral vision?
- What objects are nearby? Which are farther away?
- Listen to the sound of your breathing.
- Do you hear other noises nearby? In the distance?
- Do any sounds represent movement or direction?

That's all there is to it! This is a simple mindfulness practice to focus on your body's perceptive cues.

In the next few pages you'll read about:

- The Nature Process,
- scientific evidence of the benefits of spending time in nature,
- the emerging field of ecopsychology,
- an expansion of our five senses, and
- my motivation for sharing this information.

I offer this workbook to you as a heartfelt gift. May it inspire you to open to all your senses as you welcome your true nature and the joy of our natural world into every moment of your life!

"My initial experience with the 54 Senses was amazement! Who knew I had that many senses? As a person who lives more in her head than in her body, it is an interesting and awakening process to get in touch with more parts of who I am and to be aware of and 'feel' through more than my 'five senses.' Re-connecting with the natural world through all of my senses helps me feel nurtured, supported, cared for, and part of the greater whole. This experience helps me make better 'sense' of my life."

~ Kathy M.

The Nature Process®

"The Nature Process® shows you how to re-connect with nature and yourself in a way that will fundamentally change your life. When we live from a place of knowing that we are part of nature, we tap into the most powerful source of energy in the universe: nature itself."

~ Tabitha Jayne, creator of The Nature Process

The "54 Senses" are just one aspect, albeit the most important, of The Nature Process, which consists of five principles or steps that allow you to consciously experience and understand what happens naturally when humans are present in Nature.

The Nature Process concepts offer powerful tools to help manage stress, promote creative thinking, and improve your mental health by helping you to release grief, re-think limiting beliefs, explore and expand goal-setting options, and help clarify most any concern or decision-making process.

⊛ **Natural Presence**

Step into a deeper experience of the natural world as you become aware of your 54 Senses. Natural presence is a state of being in the moment, a sense of mindful awareness of your surroundings, and the related sensations you experience through all your senses.

❀ **Natural Body**

Your natural body is how you connect to the environment around you and process the information you receive. It is the means by which you translate the information you receive through your 54 Senses.

❀ **Natural Attraction**

Learn to think like Nature and as a part of Nature as you tap into Nature's wisdom. Use the metaphors of places you observe in nature that feel unique, interesting, beautiful, and alluring and reflect on how you also embody these same attributes.

❀ **Natural Communication**

Experience and understand the non-verbal language of Nature as you learn how you can think and act from a place of balance and wholeness.

❀ **Natural Release**

Feel yourself as a part of a greater whole, Nature, and use your sensory connections to return to a state of balance and well-being.

The Nature Process is what happens naturally when we are open enough to mindfully connect with nature and to allow ourselves to be guided by it. Tabitha has observed, on a detailed level, what happens within herself and her clients when in nature. She has clarified these intuitive steps into a simple process that can be taught to others, using the foundations of applied ecopsychology.

This workbook gives you an opportunity to actually experience each of the 54 Senses referred to in The Nature Process teachings and to do so at your own pace and in your own setting.

If you would like to experience a full session of The Nature Process, I've recorded a guided twenty-minute complimentary session. Visit www.TheNatureProcess.co and click to join the e-mail list. You will receive a link where you can listen to or download the audio file.

And for a more in-depth exploration of these concepts, I highly recommend that you purchase a copy of Tabitha Jayne's book, *The Nature Process (2nd Edition): Discover the power and potential of your natural self and improve your well-being.*

The Science behind Spending Time in Nature

There's a growing body of scientific evidence that being out in nature can:

- ❀ Decrease feelings of stress, anxiety, depression, anger, aggression, frustration, and fatigue
- ❀ Increase self-esteem, mood, vitality, creativity, and happiness
- ❀ Reduce mental exhaustion, headaches, and physical pain
- ❀ Improve academic performance and workplace productivity
- ❀ Improve sleep and support addiction recovery

For a comprehensive list of the physical and emotional benefits of spending time in nature, along with related scientific studies, visit www.TheNatureProcess.co/The-Science.

Additional topics you may wish to explore:

- ❀ **Nature deficit disorder** - a way to describe the psychological, physical, and cognitive costs of human alienation from nature, particularly for children in their vulnerable developing years. See *Last Child in the Woods* by Richard Louv.

Shinrin-Yoku – "Forest bathing" proponents in the U.S. and Japan study the benefits of bathing in the atmosphere of the forest to enhance health, wellness, and happiness. For more information, visit The Association of Nature and Forest Therapy www.natureandforesttherapy.org.

❀ ❀ ❀

"I have always been drawn to spending time in nature. Sometimes the drive is so intense I schedule my day around getting outside. It's where I go to look for answers to the questions/situations that keep me from being at peace. I now know that I have only begun to scratch the surface of the healing that's available."

~ Connie S.

54 Senses and Ecopsychology

The term "ecopsychology" was first coined in 1992 by Theodore Roszak in his book *The Voice of the Earth*. He, along with therapists, activists, ecologists, and wilderness experts explored the need for a field of study that wove together the human aspects of health, wellness, environmental activism, and psychology.

Ecopsychology is the melding of human psychology with the recognition that a vibrant, lush planet earth directly improves both the physical health and the emotional life of humans. Ecopsychology acknowledges that the health of humans and the health of the planet are intimately connected.

An Expansion of our Five Senses

Science and philosophy writer Guy Murchie described an abundance of human senses in his 1978 book, *The Seven Mysteries of Life; An Exploration in Science and Philosophy*.

After scrutinizing hundreds of scientific articles about natural senses, he concluded that there are more than eighty different biological senses and instincts, grouped into five general categories:

- Radiation Senses (sight, sun sense, temperature)
- Feeling Senses (hearing, feeling, weight, balance, space, pressure)
- Chemical Senses (smell, taste, appetite)

11

- ⚙ Mental Senses (pain, distress, fear, play, humour, sensuality, procreation, language, intuition, meditation)
- ⚙ Spiritual Senses (conscience, sorrow, love, consciousness, community)

Michael Cohen, Ph.D., Ed.D., a pioneer in the field of applied ecopsychology and founder of Project NatureConnect, expanded this work based on his experiential learning from more than twenty-six years of living and teaching outdoors. He refined Murchie's list into fifty-four distinct senses.

The 54 Senses of The Nature Process are based upon and adapted from Dr. Cohen's work.

The Nature Process identifies these six sense groups:

- ⚙ **Radiation:** ability to perceive invisible waves such as sound, light, electricity, and magnetic pull.

- ⚙ **Feeling:** physical sensations including touch, appetite, motion, weight, balance, space, pressure, and pain.

- ⚙ **Chemical:** awareness and recognition of the meaning and uses of hormones, scents, and tastes.

- ⚙ **Mental:** perception and expression of intellectual and emotional thoughts and reactions using the mind and reasoning.

- ⚙ **Communal:** innate desire to be part of a community for physical as well as emotional support and survival.

- ⚙ **Spiritual:** advanced thoughts including aesthetics, humility, ethics, as well as conscience, joy, sorrow, spirituality, and unity.

Does the number "54" represent some finite number of senses? Absolutely not! You may discover other abilities and sensitivities that would expand this list.

The more you practice being in tune with the knowledge that flows from your body to your brain, the more you'll be able to expand this list yourself!

"The Nature Process gave me access to a level of connection with nature I intuitively knew was possible, but had never experienced."

~ Steve W.

My Motivation for Sharing This Information

In 2003, I lost my older son to suicide.

Every few weeks, for years after his death, I was compelled to take my devastated heart out to nature. I furiously planted wildflowers in my woodland garden until my throbbing back begged me to stop. In defiance of the numbness in my heart, I relished the raw blisters that bubbled up as I ripped out invasive weeds. I welcomed the sting of sunburn as I hiked in the open prairie.

Some deep "knowing" told me that spending this time in nature would gently heal my heartbreak. And it did.

This journey through grief led me to become a yoga and meditation teacher. My classes and workshops offer tools to soften anguish and recognize (even welcome!) the unexpected gifts that can come from the experience of profound loss.

It wasn't easy at first to accept these gifts of compassion, non-judgment, and patience. Over the years, especially during my times in nature, I have begun to embody them more easily.

It seems that I had been practicing something akin to The Nature Process for years, I just had never defined or organized it or, to be honest, even thought about it.

This method teaches a few simple steps that anyone can use to awaken the same profound depth of healing and release that I experienced in nature.

I studied directly with Tabitha Jayne to become the first Certified Nature Process Facilitator in 2014. Now, as The Nature Process Director of Training and Development, I not only meld The Nature Process tools with my yoga and meditation teachings, I also support others to integrate its lessons into their own healing practices.

With this workbook, I invite you to find your own sense of stability, ease, and softening. Go out into nature. Reconnect to it in each moment, with every breath, and all your senses, and then notice how it changes your life.

"If facts are the seeds that later produce knowledge and wisdom, then the emotions and the impressions of the senses are the fertile soil in which the seeds must grow."

~ Rachel Carson, ***The Sense of Wonder***

How to Use this Workbook

This workbook is designed to be used by anyone with an interest in exploring their 54 Senses from an ecopsychology perspective - whether or not you have experienced a session of The Nature Process or read the book.

You can approach this workbook from different perspectives. Maybe you just want to re-connect to your memories of being in nature. Or you might imagine that you are examining your senses for a science experiment. You may see these exercises as a way to expand and enhance your spiritual journey. You'll find that the concepts and exercises in this workbook touch on all these facets of life. Be as serious or as light-hearted as you'd like about this journey, and trust that your own interpretation and intention will be just right.

If you have read The Nature Process book or attended a session of The Nature Process, this companion workbook will allow you to deepen and broaden your understanding and experience of the concept of being in a state of natural presence.

Helpful hint: If you just read these exercises without actually doing them, then you'll miss out on most of the benefits of this workbook! So follow the suggestions on each sense to make this a truly experiential exercise rather than just an intellectual one.

Begin your exploration of each sense by taking a few slow, deep breaths. Focus all your attention on the place and time; envision this as a nature-based mindfulness practice.

You can use this workbook on your own or together with others in a group. Sharing impressions and comparing notes with fellow explorers can make for an interesting and inspiring event!

The whole point of this workbook is to help you expand and enhance your perception of the senses you use every day so you become more at ease and comfortable with your relationship to the earth and the natural essences of life that surround you.

Start your adventure by working through the senses in the order they appear in the book, or pick one of the sense groupings and focus on the senses in just that one group.

Here some suggestions for when, how, and where to use this book:

When?

- ❀ You can explore one sense each day for fifty-four days, or go deeper and explore one sense each week for a year-long practice. You might choose to schedule an hour once a week and examine a few of the senses in one sitting.
- ❀ Schedule a regular time for this practice – reserve the times in your calendar as a reminder. Don't be rigid about this, but simply set an intention and a commitment.
- ❀ Ask your family or housemates to allow you this time, so you can be undisturbed.

How?

⊛ Each page has bulleted suggestions marked with a "⊛" for ways you can examine and explore the sense. Work through each concept at your own pace, but try to allow a minimum of one full minute to experience each bullet point within the exercises.

⊛ Some pages have a special section marked with "✂" that indicates activities you can do over a longer period of time or in other settings.

⊛ Some senses seem to overlap or repeat others; read the exercises carefully and you'll see there's a different emphasis or focus on each one.

⊛ Some senses touch on difficult emotions, physical pain, or harsh memories. If you feel uncomfortable working with any of the senses, please honour your primary need to be safe and comfortable with the exercises and skip any that you don't want to explore. If you are under the care of a professional for therapy or emotional support, please discuss any strong or negative reactions with them. Many people have triggers or grief that can surface when their felt senses remind them of an experience in the past. The exercises in this workbook are not intended to diagnose or treat any emotional or physical condition.

⊛ Each page has an "interesting facts" box with examples of how the sense is expressed in nature, and is listed in the "Index to Interesting Facts" at the end of the book. Do your own research about this for any topics that catch your attention. A fascinating site about nature from the Biomimicry Institute is www.AskNature.org. You may learn some surprising nature facts and how these concepts are being used to inspire products, processes, and policies for humans.

⊛ Allow for time to reflect and make notes. Fifteen to thirty minutes each session should be plenty but, again, use your own sense for how much time feels right for you. If you're comfortable with just five minutes at a session – that's a great place to start!

⊛ Each of the exercises offers questions for reflection. There are no right or wrong answers to these questions … just your honest, non-judgmental, and heartfelt reactions.

Where?

⊛ Indoors or outdoors? Use your intuition each time you begin, and then find an alluring place to settle in. Make sure the location you choose feels safe and comfortable and offers you a sense of privacy.

⊛ Gather up items that will make it easy and convenient for you to be comfortable – chair, blanket, sunglasses, beverage, etc.

⊛ If you're indoors, sit where you have a view of the outdoors or relax next to a favorite house plant.

After you've experienced all the senses on your own, treat yourself to a complimentary guided audio session from Tabitha Jayne,

"Re-Activate Your 54 Senses" at this link:

www.TheNatureProcess.co/54SensesMeditation

Reflecting on Each Sense

Because you will explore some of the senses with your eyes closed, read through all the instructions on each page before you begin.

After each exercise, there is a page for you to reflect on these questions:

❀ What physical sensations did you experience?

Take a few moments to be aware of sensations in your body both before and after exploring each sense. Make note of areas that feel open and spacious, as well as areas that feel tight, blocked or constricted.

❀ What emotions arose as you explored this sense?

Did awareness of this sense trigger any memories or feelings?

❀ What did you learn about this sense?

Did something you experienced about this sense surprise you or teach you something new?

❀ What can you do to remain aware of this sense?

What reminders can you give yourself so that you think about this sense at different times of the day, in different settings, and from different perspectives?

At the bottom of each page you can track your overall understanding of and comfort level with each sense by checking one of these boxes:

Rate this Sense: ☐ Attraction ☐ Neutral ☐ Aversion

❀ **Attraction:** overall, you found it was easy to tap into this sense and it felt good to do so.

21

⊛ **Neutral**: you were able to experience the sense but it didn't leave you with a particular emotion - neither good nor bad.

⊛ **Aversion**: either you were not able to connect or you did connect but had a negative or uncomfortable reaction to it.

If you experienced a strong aversion or negative emotional or physical reaction, please consider seeking professional help to assist you in working through the thoughts and emotions around the sense. This workbook is not intended to provide professional, therapeutic, or medical advise. Negative physical or emotional reactions can be powerful indicators of an area of your life that is ready to be explored and nutured with professional support.

After you have experienced all of the senses, you may wish to revisit those that you marked either "Neutral" or "Aversion" and delve deeper into the sense to understand your initial reaction.

What is Natural Presence?

Imagine your favorite pooch is let off-leash in the forest.

She heads towards the tree line and you observe that she seems to pause as she comes fully into the place and the moment through all her senses.

If you observe her closely, you see that her nostrils relax and then flare in an effort to drink in all scents from every direction.

Her eyes soften as if to expand her peripheral vision to perceive shape, form, design, and movement of everything in her line of sight.

Her ears perk up - not on alert so much - but more like she's fanning out her antennae to be able to receive every sound, from near and far. You imagine she could hear sounds from deep within the earth or as far away as the moon.

Her tail lifts - anther antennae it seems - but this time it's as a radio tower bringing in the electrical activity of the temperature and wind expanding all the sensations on her skin and hair. You notice even the hairs on her neck and back seem to be lifted to receive the vibrations of everything she perceives.

And then she's off, racing into the woods, with the explosion of all her other senses as they guide her to the most amazing things to nibble, chase, lick, climb, or fetch.

The very best part of the day is when she rolls around luxuriously in the remains of something that's now in an intoxicating (and really stinky) stage of decomposition - not something we humans are drawn to do!

You're amazed at how she can scramble with ease (and joy!) over uneven terrain. As she glides over logs and rocks you see that she's fully in alignment with her senses of balance and weight and gravity.

And she is 100% in this moment. This sweet (and smelly) pooch embodies natural presence!

Are you ready to join her in fully experiencing each moment of being in Nature?

❀ ❀ ❀

"I only went out for a walk, and finally concluded to stay out till sundown, for going out, I found, was really going in."

**~ John of the mountains:
the unpublished journals of John Muir**

Introductory Exercise REFLECTIONS:

_____

_____

_____

_____

_____

_____

_____

_____

_____

_____

_____

_____

_____

_____

_____

_____

_____

_____

_____

_____

_____

_____

_____

_____

_____

_____

_____

_____

_____

Introductory Exercise

Settle into a quiet place where you feel comfortable and safe. Note your mood, thoughts, and any physical sensations before you begin.

Read through the suggestions on this page then close your eyes.

Remember a time when you had a memorable experience in nature.

- ❀ Allow the memory to build as you remember the sensations through each of the five senses you are most familiar with – sight, smell, taste, sound, and touch.
- ❀ Think of what you were doing and how you interacted with the nature around you.
- ❀ How does it make you feel to re-experience this memory?
- ❀ Note any changes in your mood, thoughts, or physical sensations compared to when you first started this exercise and then open your eyes.

Write your reflections on the page to the left, then turn the page and begin with Sense #1.

Radiation Senses

What physical sensations did you experience?

_____

_____

_____

_____

_____

What emotions arose as you explored this sense?

_____

_____

_____

_____

_____

What did you learn about this sense?

_____

_____

_____

_____

_____

What can you do to remain aware of this sense?

_____

_____

_____

_____

_____

Rate this Sense: ☐ Attraction   ☐ Neutral   ☐ Aversion

Sense of light and sight (#1)

❀ Spend a few minutes staring at a natural setting and allow your sense of light and sight to absorb the scene. How does it make you feel?

❀ Based on the light, can you tell what time of day it is?

❀ Notice the light as it's filtered through leaves, in shadow, or when it reflects off water or other objects. How does filtered, shadowed, or reflected light feel compared to unobstructed light?

❀ Widen your peripheral vision. Without moving your eyes, what can you see at the upper range of your field of vision? The bottom, the left, and the right?

❀ What light catches your eye? Why?

❀ How does the light feel on your face and body?

✂ Explore this sense at different times of day and night.

✂ Select one object that you can see easily as you go through your normal day. Look at the light on and around this object as often as you can over 24 hours. How does the light change?

> The amount of uninterrupted darkness (photoperiodism) determines the formation of flowers on many plants. "Short-day" plants like poinsettias require at least 12 hours of darkness to bloom. "Long Day" plants like California poppies require at least 12 hours of light to bloom. Asters require both: long-day (summertime growth) followed by short-day (autumn blooms).

29

What physical sensations did you experience?

_____

_____

_____

_____

_____

What emotions arose as you explored this sense?

_____

_____

_____

_____

_____

What did you learn about this sense?

_____

_____

_____

_____

_____

What can you do to remain aware of this sense?

_____

_____

_____

_____

_____

Rate this Sense: ☐ Attraction ☐ Neutral ☐ Aversion

Sense of seeing without eyes (i.e. heliotropism) (#2)

Close your eyes as you try each of these activities:

⊛ How does it feel to have your eyes closed while you're awake?

⊛ Notice the sensation where the upper lids touch the lower lids.

⊛ Notice your eyeballs behind your closed lids as you move your eyes around.

⊛ Soften the muscles around your forehead and notice if you see colours, shading, or patterns in your inner gaze.

⊛ Listen for a sound; orient your head towards it.

⊛ Move your eyes towards the brightest light.

     o Turn your head towards it then orient your whole body towards the bright light.

     o Open your eyes to view what it is that is so bright in your awareness.

⊛ Close your eyes again and move your eyes to focus towards the darkest area and follow the same steps.

Heliotropism is also known as "solar tracking". The leaves of the *silphium laciniatum* plants orient themselves in a north to south direction to avoid the direct rays of the midday sun, thus leading to the plant's common name, compass plant.

What physical sensations did you experience?

_____

_____

_____

_____

_____

What emotions arose as you explored this sense?

_____

_____

_____

_____

_____

What did you learn about this sense?

_____

_____

_____

_____

_____

What can you do to remain aware of this sense?

_____

_____

_____

_____

_____

Rate this Sense: ☐ Attraction ☐ Neutral ☐ Aversion

Sense of colour (#3)

- ❀ Look around you, near and far, and notice all the colours.
- ❀ What physical sensations are activated through your eyes, forehead, and brain as you tune into the colours?
- ❀ Count the number of distinct colours you see.
- ❀ Say each colour's name out loud.
- ❀ Look at each colour again, more closely, and notice the gradients of colour and shading.
- ❀ Which colours feel light & airy?
- ❀ Which feel heavy & dark?
- ❀ Which are warm and welcoming?
- ❀ Which are cold or harsh?
- ❀ Which colours do you want to touch?
- ❀ Which do you NOT want to touch?

Butterflies respond to the color of the petals to find nectar. "Nectar guides" are patterns on flowers that guide pollinators to their nectar. The color of the nectar guide of the horse chestnut tree (*Aesculus hippocastanum*) changes from yellow to red when nectar is no longer in production. Butterflies tend to avoid the color green when feeding, but are attracted to it during egg laying.

What physical sensations did you experience?

_____

_____

_____

_____

_____

What emotions arose as you explored this sense?

_____

_____

_____

_____

_____

What did you learn about this sense?

_____

_____

_____

_____

_____

What can you do to remain aware of this sense?

_____

_____

_____

_____

_____

Rate this Sense: ☐ Attraction ☐ Neutral ☐ Aversion

Sensitivity to radiation other than visible light (i.e. radio waves and X-rays) (#4)

- ⚘ Remember when you had an X-ray, MRI, CAT scan, or went through an airport security scan. How did it make you feel?
- ⚘ Notice your level of brain activity after an extended period of watching TV or working on the computer.
- ✺ According to the World Health Organization, computers generate levels of radiation that can impact our well-being. Recommendations:
    - ✺ Unplug any devices in your home that do not need to be plugged in and move cellular and electronic devices away from your bed.
    - ✺ Arrange your desk so that when you are not working at your computer, you maintain a distance of at least 18 inches from it.
    - ✺ Pay attention to how you feel when you are near electronic devices.

Controversial scientific studies around the site of the Chernobyl fallout zone show mammal diversity and abundance equal to that of a protected nature reserve, with rare species including bears, lynx, river otter, and badger. Bird diversity includes 61 rare species. Whooper swans—never before reported in the region—now appear regularly. What's the controversy? Some attribute this wealth of animal life to lack of human activity in the area.

What physical sensations did you experience?

_____

_____

_____

_____

_____

What emotions arose as you explored this sense?

_____

_____

_____

_____

_____

What did you learn about this sense?

_____

_____

_____

_____

_____

What can you do to remain aware of this sense?

_____

_____

_____

_____

_____

Rate this Sense: ☐ Attraction ☐ Neutral ☐ Aversion

Sense of hearing (includes resonance, vibrations, sonar, and ultrasonic frequencies) (#5)

- Sit outside and tune into your sense of hearing.
    - Notice what happens to your physical body when you consciously pay attention to your sense of hearing and sound.
    - Notice what sounds are nearest to you; which are farther away; which are louder or softer.
    - What causes each sound?
    - What is the musical tone, pitch, vibration, rhythm, or frequency of each sound?
    - Is there an underlying background noise?
    - Visit this same site at different times of the day and notice if there are changes in the sounds.
- Remember a time you were under water and reflect on the deep silence you noticed then.
- Remember the differences in the sensation of sound under water in a bathtub, the ocean, a river, or swimming pool.

> Owls rely on their hearing when hunting. They can differentiate between sounds that move horizontally and sounds that move vertically, a phenomenon first noted by Ivan Pavlov. Researchers mapped which auditory neurons in owls' brains fired in response to sounds and found that owls basically have a topographic map of space in their brains.

What physical sensations did you experience?

_____

_____

_____

_____

_____

What emotions arose as you explored this sense?

_____

_____

_____

_____

_____

What did you learn about this sense?

_____

_____

_____

_____

_____

What can you do to remain aware of this sense?

_____

_____

_____

_____

_____

Rate this Sense: ☐ Attraction ☐ Neutral ☐ Aversion

Electromagnetic sense and polarity within the body; ability to generate current as in the nervous system and brain waves (#6)

⚘ Did you know you have an energy field that sends electric current through your body? You can experience this: rub your palms together briskly for about a full minute. When they feel very warm, slowly separate your hands just a half-inch or so, and notice the sensation of a magnetic pull that draws the hands together. Experiment with moving your hands farther apart until you no longer feel the pull.

⚘ Breathe in and imagine the life force (also known as spirit, prana, chi, or Ki) that comes in on the air. Imagine it flowing to every living cell in your body.

⚘ Imagine you've touched an electrical outlet; how would it feel in your body?

⚘ How would it feel to share energy with another living entity? Situate yourself close to a large tree. Imagine that your electrical energy field could merge with the electrical energy field of the tree.

Scientists have found that plants can conduct electricity: researchers discovered that big leaf maple trees generated a steady voltage of up to a few hundred millivolts. With a booster converter, they were able to generate enough voltage to run low-power sensors.

What physical sensations did you experience?

_____

_____

_____

_____

_____

What emotions arose as you explored this sense?

_____

_____

_____

_____

What did you learn about this sense?

_____

_____

_____

_____

What can you do to remain aware of this sense?

_____

_____

_____

_____

Rate this Sense: ☐ Attraction ☐ Neutral ☐ Aversion

Sense of electromagnetic fields outside the body (#7)

❀ Read the exercises in sense #6 "Electromagnetic sense and polarity within the body" and visualise this same energy field around everything you see.

    ○ Imagine how it would feel to expand this energetic awareness out to the entire earth, planets, and stars.

    ○ How would you describe your awareness of these external electromagnetic fields as compared to internal fields?

❀ Walk around your house – inside and outside.

    ○ Notice electric outlets and other magnetic lines that connect to the building.

    ○ Stand by the electrical box or utility box. How does it feel to be near these lines? What do you notice about them?

❀ Imagine that you are a sea turtle and use the electromagnetic fields of the earth to navigate over long distances. What skills might you use to do this?

Herds of cows and deer align themselves with magnetic north shown in 8,510 images from Google Earth of grazing and resting cattle in 308 pastures around the world. This same phenomenon is found among herds of 2,974 wild deer in 277 locations across the Czech Republic.

What physical sensations did you experience?

_____

_____

_____

_____

_____

What emotions arose as you explored this sense?

_____

_____

_____

_____

_____

What did you learn about this sense?

_____

_____

_____

_____

_____

What can you do to remain aware of this sense?

_____

_____

_____

_____

_____

Rate this Sense: ☐ Attraction   ☐ Neutral   ☐ Aversion

Awareness of temperature (#8)

- ❀ Stay inside your house and notice the temperature.
    - o How does the temperature of the air feel on your skin?
    - o In your nostrils, sinuses, throat, lungs and belly as you inhale and exhale?
- ❀ Go outside and notice the temperature there, using the same questions from above.
- ❀ Go inside/then outside a few times. Each time, compare the physical sensations of temperature in these two locations.
- ✄ Adjust your indoor temperature throughout the day: open/close windows, change the setting on the thermostat, or put on a sweater and take it off.
    - ✄ Tune into how the temperature feels to your physical body.
    - ✄ How does each temperature affect your level of concentration?
    - ✄ How does it affect your mood?

> On cool days, honey bees cluster together to keep the temperature in the hive's nursery between 91°F and 97°F to protect the brood. On hot days, they cool the hive by fanning their wings or by spreading water on the comb to remove heat through evaporation. They rarely allow the temperature to vary more than 2°F in the brood area over the course of a day.

What physical sensations did you experience?

_____

_____

_____

_____

_____

What emotions arose as you explored this sense?

_____

_____

_____

_____

_____

What did you learn about this sense?

_____

_____

_____

_____

_____

What can you do to remain aware of this sense?

_____

_____

_____

_____

_____

Rate this Sense: ☐ Attraction ☐ Neutral ☐ Aversion

Awareness of weather (#9)

❀ Either go to a nearby window or go outside.

　　○ Pay attention to the wind, temperature, clouds in the sky, moisture in the air, and the air pressure around you.

　　○ How would you describe the weather?

　　○ What does your observation of all these elements tell you about the weather and its likelihood of change?

　　○ Expand and explore the cues in your body and your other senses that let you know if the weather is changing.

❀ Close your eyes and remember the smell of an impending rainfall or snowstorm.

❀ Remember the sensations immediately after a heavy rainstorm ends or right when a snowfall stops.

� Go outside before, during and after a rainstorm and pay attention to the wind, temperature, clouds, humidity, and air pressure.

✖ Notice your mood with each weather change.

During the winter, wasps will all die off except for the queen; she will start a new colony from scratch in the spring.

Hedgehogs wind themselves up tightly in a ball and fall asleep in the deep mounds of leaves to take their winter nap but only after gorging themselves with fruit.

Feeling Senses

What physical sensations did you experience?

_____

_____

_____

_____

_____

What emotions arose as you explored this sense?

_____

_____

_____

_____

_____

What did you learn about this sense?

_____

_____

_____

_____

_____

What can you do to remain aware of this sense?

_____

_____

_____

_____

_____

Rate this Sense: ☐ Attraction ☐ Neutral ☐ Aversion

Sense of touch (especially on the skin) (#10)

- ✤ With your eyes, open, examine the skin on your body.
- ✤ Notice what body parts are touching something else (like your clothing) and which are touching the air.
- ✤ With your bare hands or feet, touch various objects and compare and contrast any physical and emotional sensations that you notice.
- ✤ Touch items that are opposites – such as a hot beverage and then a cold one, a rough object then a smooth one, etc. - and notice how each feels.
- ✤ Close your eyes and
  - o Remember a loving touch you've received.
  - o Remember a comforting or supportive touch.
  - o Remember a sense of pain – a cut or bruise.
  - o Remember the feel of the following sensations on your skin: the sun, the winter cold, water, a strong wind, rainfall, a warm blanket, a thorn, sunburn.

Mimosa pudica (sensitive plant) folds up its leaves when they are touched as a result of internal movement of water. Touch or air movement trigger certain areas of the stem to release chemicals, which cause water to move out of cell vacuoles and leads to cell collapse. This rapid plant movement is thought to act as a defense against being eaten.

What physical sensations did you experience?

_____

_____

_____

_____

_____

What emotions arose as you explored this sense?

_____

_____

_____

_____

_____

What did you learn about this sense?

_____

_____

_____

_____

_____

What can you do to remain aware of this sense?

_____

_____

_____

_____

_____

Rate this Sense: ☐ Attraction ☐ Neutral ☐ Aversion

Sense of seasonal changes (#11)

- Go outside and notice the plants, grasses, and trees.
    - What is the season? How do you know this?
    - How does this current season feel, physically and emotionally?
    - What is your level of energy and vitality in this season?
- Imagine that you are in this same place in each of the four seasons.
    - How would the appearance of the plants & trees differ in each?
    - How does each season feel to you, physically?
    - What would your level of energy and vitality be in each season?
    - What activities do you like to do in each?
    - What emotional differences do you notice between the seasons?
- What season do you love and look forward to? Why?
- What season do you often wish would end sooner? Why?

Annual plants' entire life cycle occurs within one growth season
– roots, stems, leaves, blossoms, seeds – and then they die.
Biennial plants live their entire life cycle within two years; roots
and leaves in the first year, then stem, flowers, blossoms, and
seeds the second year, and then they die. Perennial plants do not
die but produce stems, blossoms, fruit, and seeds each year and
may go dormant in freezing or dry weather, leaving only living
roots in the soil.

What physical sensations did you experience?

_____

_____

_____

_____

_____

What emotions arose as you explored this sense?

_____

_____

_____

_____

_____

What did you learn about this sense?

_____

_____

_____

_____

_____

What can you do to remain aware of this sense?

_____

_____

_____

_____

_____

Rate this Sense: ☐ Attraction ☐ Neutral ☐ Aversion

Awareness of pressure, particularly underground, underwater, and to wind and air (#12)

❀ Remember a time when you were under water:

    ○ Remember the sense of pressure on your physical body – from the outside as well as the inside of your body.

    ○ As you came out of the water, how did the change of pressure feel?

❀ Go outside (or remember a day) when you could feel the pressure of a really strong wind against your body. What were your physical and emotional reactions to the strong wind?

❀ Imagine that you are sitting in the centre of a tornado, within the stillness. How would it feel to move into and back out of the vortex of air around you?

❀ Visualise the heaviness of the air in a tropical rainforest; compare to the sensations of the reduced air pressure at the top of a mountain in winter.

Hurricanes are formed by changes in air pressure and temperature. A system of clouds and wind spins and grows. When the winds in the storm reach 39 mph, it is called a "tropical storm." When the wind speeds reach 74 mph, it is officially a "tropical cyclone," or hurricane.

What physical sensations did you experience?

_____

_____

_____

_____

_____

What emotions arose as you explored this sense?

_____

_____

_____

_____

_____

What did you learn about this sense?

_____

_____

_____

_____

What can you do to remain aware of this sense?

_____

_____

_____

_____

_____

Rate this Sense: ☐ Attraction ☐ Neutral ☐ Aversion

Sensitivity to gravity (#13)

- Find a secluded spot outdoors where you won't be observed.
    - o Stand up and lift one foot off the ground.
    - o Notice the sensation of gravity tugging at your lifted foot as you drop it and lift it again.
- Jump and note the sensation of your body lifting away from gravity. Observe the sensations as you return to the earth.
- Look up at the sky and focus on or visualise a cloud. How might it feel, physically, to be the cloud; to be nearly weightless? What would your relationship be with objects around you and with gravity?
- Look around you at water, rocks, trees, and earth and imagine you are each of those objects. How would your relationship to gravity feel if you were each of these objects?
- Go inside and lie down with your back on the floor. Study the layout of the ceiling and imagine you could walk on the walls or ceiling. How does this affect your awareness of the pull of gravity?

An astronaut's switch to weightlessness and back can be tough on the body. In the absence of gravity, muscles atrophy and bones lose bone mass. According to NASA, astronauts can lose 1 percent of their bone mass per month in space.

What physical sensations did you experience?

_____

_____

_____

_____

_____

What emotions arose as you explored this sense?

_____

_____

_____

_____

_____

What did you learn about this sense?

_____

_____

_____

_____

_____

What can you do to remain aware of this sense?

_____

_____

_____

_____

_____

Rate this Sense: ☐ Attraction ☐ Neutral ☐ Aversion

Sense of appetite or hunger for food, water and air (#14)

- Notice your appetite and level of thirst right now.
  - Compare that to sensations of hunger and thirst when you first wake up in the morning.
  - Compare it to the sensations you have when you have had too much to eat or drink.
- Remember how it feels, physically as well as emotionally, to be really, really hungry?
- Take a deep inhalation and hold your breath until you notice the inclination to exhale. What was the sensation, physically as well as emotionally, before you released the breath?
- Take a full exhalation and hold your breath out until you notice the inclination to inhale. What was the sensation, physically as well as emotionally before you inhaled?
- For the next few days, drink a glass of water when you first wake up and notice any reaction in your body. What sensations do you feel, physically and emotionally, as you swallow it?

> The blue whale (our largest living mammal) eats up to 8,000 pounds of food each day. The African elephant eats up to 660 pounds of food and drinks about 50 gallons of water daily. A hummingbird consumes up to eight times its body weight in one day.

What physical sensations did you experience?

_____

_____

_____

_____

_____

What emotions arose as you explored this sense?

_____

_____

_____

_____

_____

What did you learn about this sense?

_____

_____

_____

_____

What can you do to remain aware of this sense?

_____

_____

_____

_____

_____

Rate this Sense: ☐ Attraction ☐ Neutral ☐ Aversion

Sense of excretion (includes releasing toxins, waste elimination, protection from enemies, and marking territory) (#15)

- In the wild, some animals eliminate waste as a way to mark territory and confuse other animals that would attack them. Visualise how your body eliminates waste through your bladder and bowels as well as by sneezing, coughing, and sweating.
  - How does your body notify you that it is ready to eliminate waste?
  - How does it feel before and afterwards?
- Remember a time when you have "marked your territory," either literally or figuratively. Why did you do this? How did you do this?
- Have you ever had food poisoning or another illness or virus that caused you to vomit? How did the sense of "purging" feel?
- Have you ever experienced a detox cleanse? Why did you do this? How did you feel afterwards? Would you do it again?

Honey bees will not defecate inside the hive but in the winter, there may only be a few days warm enough to fly outside for their "cleansing flights." When the temperature warms to about 55°F thousands of bees will fly out 3-4 feet away from the hive opening and deposit a big yellow mess of bee poop.

What physical sensations did you experience?

_____

_____

_____

_____

_____

What emotions arose as you explored this sense?

_____

_____

_____

_____

_____

What did you learn about this sense?

_____

_____

_____

_____

What can you do to remain aware of this sense?

_____

_____

_____

_____

Rate this Sense: ☐ Attraction   ☐ Neutral   ☐ Aversion

Sense of weight and balance (#16)

- ⊛ Weight:
    - ⊛ Assess your physical weight in comparison to objects around you.
    - ⊛ Imagine that you're in an airplane: what would be the sensation of your physical weight?
    - ⊛ Was there a time when you felt that you carried the weight of the world on your shoulders?
- ⊛ Balance:
    - ⊛ Stand up. Bring awareness to your feet and notice how they feel against the ground. Remove your shoes & socks and notice these same sensations with your bare feet.
    - ⊛ Stand on your tiptoes and notice your balance.
    - ⊛ Shift your weight and balance on your heels.
    - ⊛ Raise one leg off the ground; place it down, then raise the other one. Do you feel more balanced on one leg vs. the other?
    - ⊛ What in your life feels out of balance? What aspects are in balance?
- ✖ What steps could you take to bring more balance to various aspects of your life?

A human weighing 130 lbs. on earth would weigh 49.1 lbs. on Mercury, 117.9 lbs. on Venus, 307.3 lbs. on Jupiter, 21.6 lbs. on the moon, and 3,519.3 lbs. on the sun.

What physical sensations did you experience?

_____

_____

_____

_____

_____

What emotions arose as you explored this sense?

_____

_____

_____

_____

_____

What did you learn about this sense?

_____

_____

_____

_____

_____

What can you do to remain aware of this sense?

_____

_____

_____

_____

_____

Rate this Sense: ☐ Attraction ☐ Neutral ☐ Aversion

Space or proximity sense (#17)

Awareness of your position in space, and of each of your body parts in relation to the rest of your body, is known as "proprioception." This awareness operates unconsciously from sense receptors in your muscles, joints, tendons, and the balance organ of the inner ear.

⊛ Imagine that you are looking at a map and describe where you are. What is nearby? What is far away?
- Imagine you are looking at your location on a globe and answer the same questions.
- Imagine that you are looking at your location from Mars and answer the same questions.
- Notice an object that is near you and move closer to it, then move farther away and notice how it feels when you come into and move out of proximity to the object.
- Look around you for a moment then close your eyes and sense objects that are within arm's reach.
- How does it feel when someone is "in your space?"

✂ For the next day, notice the amount of space you leave between yourself and others. How does it feel if that distance is closer or farther away than you would like?

Some plants are aware of the space around them. By analyzing the ratio of red light and far red light (light at the far end of the spectrum) falling on their leaves, plants can sense the presence of other plants nearby and try to grow the other direction.

What physical sensations did you experience?

_____

_____

_____

_____

_____

What emotions arose as you explored this sense?

_____

_____

_____

_____

_____

What did you learn about this sense?

_____

_____

_____

_____

_____

What can you do to remain aware of this sense?

_____

_____

_____

_____

_____

Rate this Sense: ☐ Attraction ☐ Neutral ☐ Aversion

Sense of motion; body movement sensations, and sense of mobility (#18)

❁ Watch Pharrell Williams' "Happy" video:
https://www.youtube.com/watch?v=y6Sxv-sUYtM

  o As you listen to the music, move your body in time to the rhythm.

  o How does it feel as you move or dance?

  o Close your eyes while you move – does it feel different than with your eyes open?

❁ Remember a time when your physical movements were restricted; how did that feel?

❁ Go outside and notice:

  o Moving objects - notice their speed, direction, and pattern and try to determine what causes the movement.

  o Focus on a large rock and imagine it over eons of time. Would there be discernible movement or change due to weather, water, or wind?

  o Do you hear any sounds that indicate movement?

The Mangrove Rivulus fish has been shown to jump out of the water to get away from predators and then jump back in. They flip head-over-tail across land to travel to wet leaves, small puddles, and crab burrows, while "breathing" through their skin.

65

What physical sensations did you experience?

_____

_____

_____

_____

_____

What emotions arose as you explored this sense?

_____

_____

_____

_____

_____

What did you learn about this sense?

_____

_____

_____

_____

_____

What can you do to remain aware of this sense?

_____

_____

_____

_____

_____

Rate this Sense: ☐ Attraction ☐ Neutral ☐ Aversion

Coriolis sense or awareness of effects of the rotation of the earth (#19)

- Imagine you can do a super-human jump, high into the earth's atmosphere.
    - o What would you notice if you looked down and saw the earth rotating?
    - o Notice that you would land back on earth in a different location.
    - o Jump up and down a few times and get the sense of the earth rotating beneath you.
- Watch this video about the coriolis effect. What happens when you throw a ball while riding on a merry-go-round? http://video.nationalgeographic.com/tv/none-of-the-above/coriolis-effect
- Watch this video of the coriolis effect on water at the equator: https://youtu.be/Kk7sXkzmtp0
- Notice the position of the sun every hour throughout an entire day and think about why it appears to be in a different location since the last time you looked at it.
- Select an outdoor object that is in full sun. Observe the sun and shadows on this object every hour for one day.

> Hurricanes cannot form along or near the equator because the Coriolis Effect is at its weakest there. Hurricanes need a strong spinning motion in order to form.

What physical sensations did you experience?

_____

_____

_____

_____

_____

What emotions arose as you explored this sense?

_____

_____

_____

_____

_____

What did you learn about this sense?

_____

_____

_____

_____

_____

What can you do to remain aware of this sense?

_____

_____

_____

_____

_____

Rate this Sense: ☐ Attraction   ☐ Neutral   ☐ Aversion

Sense of physical pain (#20)

⊕ What is the most painful event that's ever happened to your body?

    ○ Where did you feel this pain in your body?

    ○ Is this pain now chronic or did it eventually go away?

    ○ What emotions arise when you think about this pain?

⊕ Answer these questions about your pain:

    ○ How did you cope with this? What did you do to overcome the pain or is it still there?

    ○ Did you have to change aspects of your life to be able to function with this pain? If so, what did you change?

    ○ What level of support did you have from others during this time?

    ○ Is there anything you learned from dealing with these painful experiences that you could apply to enhance and support current painful issues in your life or to support others?

Neuroscientists from multiple universities have devised an objective way to measure physical pain as well as social (emotional) pain using functional magnetic resonance imaging (fMRI). They discovered that the patterns (neurologic signatures) in question are transferable across different people, allowing them to predict pain intensity with over 95% accuracy. Their findings appear in the New England Journal of Medicine.

What physical sensations did you experience?

_____

_____

_____

_____

_____

What emotions arose as you explored this sense?

_____

_____

_____

_____

_____

What did you learn about this sense?

_____

_____

_____

_____

_____

What can you do to remain aware of this sense?

_____

_____

_____

_____

_____

Rate this Sense: ☐ Attraction ☐ Neutral ☐ Aversion

Sense of emotions (includes happiness, distress, joy, contentment, pain, and grief) (#21)

- ❀ Remember moments of intense joy and absolute contentment.
    - o Do you remember a place in your body where you held the emotions of those moments?
    - o How do they feel in your body now?
    - o What happens to your breath when you remember those times?
- ❀ Remember a time in the past when you were in a period of stress, grief, or remorse and answer the same questions from above.
    - o What actions helped you move into a more balanced mental state?
    - o In hindsight, was there any silver lining that came because of this period in your life?
- ❀ What's an uncomfortable personal or professional challenge that you're facing right now?
    - o How is this affecting you physically?
    - o How is this affecting your life and relationships?
    - o How is this affecting your work?
    - o What actions could you take to become more comfortable with this challenge?

Go to a Forest. Walk slowly. Breathe. Open all your senses.
This is the healing way of Shinrin-Yoku Forest Therapy,
the medicine of simply being in the forest.

What physical sensations did you experience?

_____

_____

_____

_____

_____

What emotions arose as you explored this sense?

_____

_____

_____

_____

_____

What did you learn about this sense?

_____

_____

_____

_____

_____

What can you do to remain aware of this sense?

_____

_____

_____

_____

_____

Rate this Sense: ☐ Attraction ☐ Neutral ☐ Aversion

Sense of fear, dread of injury, death, or attack (#22)

❀ What do you not do because you are afraid of injury or death?

❀ The expression, *"Today is a good day to die,"* is attributed to Oglala Chief Low Dog as he led his tribe into battle with General Custer. What does this quote mean to you?

❀ Imagine you have just been told you only have one year to live.

  o How would you spend your last year on earth?

  o What would be your priorities?

  o What things would be unimportant for you?

  o How does thinking about your death affect your perspective on your life?

❀ Remember a time when you were fearful.

  o How did your body and breath respond?

  o Did you go into the "fight, flight, or flee" response? In what way?

  o How did you come back to your everyday mental state after the threat passed?

The mimic octopus can change its form to resemble that of other marine organisms to scare off possible predators. Mimicking is common in animals for defense, but this one is *much* more dynamic. It can change its body shape and behaviour to resemble a number of species, including sea-snakes, jellyfish, lion fish, and more.

What physical sensations did you experience?

_____

_____

_____

_____

_____

What emotions arose as you explored this sense?

_____

_____

_____

_____

_____

What did you learn about this sense?

_____

_____

_____

_____

_____

What can you do to remain aware of this sense?

_____

_____

_____

_____

_____

Rate this Sense: ☐ Attraction ☐ Neutral ☐ Aversion

Sense of pupation (includes dormancy, cocoon-building, and metamorphosis) (#23)

⊛ Close your eyes and visualise wintertime.

    o   Open all your senses to an awareness of winter.

    o   How does the sense of winter affect your activities, decisions, need to pupate, hibernate, or metamorphose into a new you?

    o   Visualise each of the other three seasons and explore the same question.

⊛ Remember a time when you went into a period of emotional or intellectual dormancy or hibernation.

    o   What did you do to accomplish this and how did it feel?

    o   Why did you go into this state?

    o   What brought you out of that state?

⊛ Remember a time when you felt that you were metaphorically pupating, cocooning, or metamorphosing into something new.

    o   How did each stage feel – physically and emotionally?

    o   What stage are you in right now?

At birth a kangaroo baby, called a joey, is just 0.2 to 0.9 inches (the size of a grain of rice or bee). It crawls to its mother's pouch to nurse and gestates from 4 to 15 months. A mother kangaroo can suckle two joeys at different developmental stages at the same time with milk that has different nutritional content.

What physical sensations did you experience?

_____

_____

_____

_____

_____

What emotions arose as you explored this sense?

_____

_____

_____

_____

_____

What did you learn about this sense?

_____

_____

_____

_____

_____

What can you do to remain aware of this sense?

_____

_____

_____

_____

_____

Rate this Sense: ☐ Attraction ☐ Neutral ☐ Aversion

Urge to hunt and gather food (#24)

- ❀ Remember a time when you picked your own food from the garden or gathered berries or mushrooms in the wild. How did these experiences make you feel?

- ❀ What thoughts and feelings arise when you think about the following topics?

  - o Have you ever hunted or fished for your own food or known someone who has?

  - o Have you allowed someone else to kill for food on your behalf?

  - o Imagine eating food that was raised and slaughtered humanely vs. eating food that was raised and slaughtered in a factory farm.

  - o Imagine eating fruits and vegetables grown without insecticides or pesticides vs. eating foods that were grown with chemicals.

- ❀ What is your personal statement pertaining to humanitarian and environmental methods for raising the food that you eat?

- ✖ For the next few days, read labels and ask questions to learn about the foods you eat, where the food came from, and how it was raised or farmed.

The slippery rim and inner walls of the carnivorous pitcher plant helps insects to fall into the digestive fluid at the bottom of the deep trap. Nutrients are absorbed from this insect "soup."

Chemical Senses

What physical sensations did you experience?

_____

_____

_____

_____

_____

What emotions arose as you explored this sense?

_____

_____

_____

_____

_____

What did you learn about this sense?

_____

_____

_____

_____

_____

What can you do to remain aware of this sense?

_____

_____

_____

_____

_____

Rate this Sense: ☐ Attraction ☐ Neutral ☐ Aversion

Sense of smell (#25)

- Sniff in through your nose multiple times in rapid succession until you need to exhale. Repeat this a few times.
  - Notice any aromas that surround you.
  - Flare your nostrils as you inhale and imagine you could breathe in everything you see around you.
  - What is the physical sensation of smelling and sniffing?
- Imagine that you are inhaling the scent of the most beautiful blossom you've ever seen. How does your breath change as you inhale?
- Remember a particular aroma that has an emotional memory for you.
- What are your favourite and least favourite smells? Try to remember each one and how they make you feel.
- For the next few days, be aware of any aromas that you notice.

> Bees distinguish between rewarding and non-rewarding flowers (amount of nectar and pollen) through scent marks left by previous bee visitors. When a bee finishes sipping nectar and gathering pollen, it leaves a scent-mark that lasts up to 60 minutes, giving the plant time to produce more nectar. This helps the next bee to not waste energy visiting flowers that have just been drained of nectar.

What physical sensations did you experience?

_____

_____

_____

_____

_____

What emotions arose as you explored this sense?

_____

_____

_____

_____

_____

What did you learn about this sense?

_____

_____

_____

_____

_____

What can you do to remain aware of this sense?

_____

_____

_____

_____

_____

Rate this Sense: ☐ Attraction ☐ Neutral ☐ Aversion

Sense of taste (#26)

- Gently inhale through your open mouth and notice the sensation of taste on your tongue.
- Remember the last meal you ate and visualise the physical sensations of tasting, biting, chewing, drinking, and swallowing.
- Remember the sensations in your mouth of crunch, melting, temperature, sweetness, spiciness, bitterness, and sourness.
- What parts of your body are involved in your sense of taste?
- What are your favourite foods and beverages? Try to remember each one and how they make you feel.
- What are your least favourite foods? Why?
- Look around. What do you imagine the taste would be for each object you see?
- What can you do to bring more flavourful foods into your life?
- For the next day, slow down as you eat and really tune into the sensations of taste.

The average person has about 10,000 taste buds. A catfish has more than 100,000 taste receptors all over its body, including the fins, back and tail. Chickens have only 24 taste buds. An octopus has 10,000 taste receptors on each sucker with 200 suckers on each of its eight arms. A butterfly's taste receptors are on its feet & legs.

What physical sensations did you experience?

_____

_____

_____

_____

_____

What emotions arose as you explored this sense?

_____

_____

_____

_____

_____

What did you learn about this sense?

_____

_____

_____

_____

_____

What can you do to remain aware of this sense?

_____

_____

_____

_____

_____

Rate this Sense: ☐ Attraction ☐ Neutral ☐ Aversion

Sense of humidity and moisture (#27)

- Go outside and notice the air against your skin and in your nostrils.
    - How would you describe the humidity level?
    - Imagine how the air would feel in the dry heat of the desert.
    - Imagine the air in a tropical rainforest.
- Does the humidity affect how straight or curly your hair is? What else does humidity affect?
- Go outside in the rain or remember a time that you did. How would the level of humidity feel in your nostrils and against your skin as the rain fell on you?
- Visualise a raindrop just being formed in a cloud, and imagine its path from the cloud to the earth.
- How would it feel if you were a cloud? What sensations would that level of humidity bring?
- Notice a plant or tree near you and visualise how its roots and leaves receive and absorb rainfall and moisture.
- Over the next few days, notice the soil around plants and trees and see if you can determine the level of moisture of the soil even before you touch it.

> Camels can survive months without a drop of water and giraffes can go weeks, but that's nothing compared to the Kangaroo Rat which lives up to 10 years and never drinks water.

What physical sensations did you experience?

_____

_____

_____

_____

_____

What emotions arose as you explored this sense?

_____

_____

_____

_____

_____

What did you learn about this sense?

_____

_____

_____

_____

What can you do to remain aware of this sense?

_____

_____

_____

_____

_____

Rate this Sense: ☐ Attraction ☐ Neutral ☐ Aversion

Hormonal sense (as to pheromones and other chemical stimuli) (#28)

◉ Think about the various hormones that have operated within your body since before birth and visualise the affect hormones have had on you.

  o Birth – pregnancy and childbirth hormones

  o Childhood – growth hormones, appetite

  o Puberty – sex and reproduction hormones

  o Aging – bone density, diabetes, menopause

◉ To experience some of the effects of hormones on the body, bring your attention to the notch at the base of your throat and visualise your thyroid located just under the skin there. Imagine how your body would feel if you had low thyroid function:

  o Fatigue, weakness, muscle aches, constipation, weight gain, dry skin, depression, memory loss

  o Visualise an over-active thyroid: rapid heartbeat, sweating, shaky hands, weight loss, difficulty sleeping, brittle hair

---

A honeybee releases an alarm pheromone when it senses danger or stings an animal. This scent attracts other bees to the location and causes the other bees to attack. Beekeepers use smokers (burning pine needles, cardboard, fabric, or some types of leaves in a metal container with a bellows to produce smoke) to mask the scent of the alarm pheromone and trigger a feeding frenzy to keep the bees from attacking when their hives are inspected or honey is removed.

What physical sensations did you experience?

_____

_____

_____

_____

_____

What emotions arose as you explored this sense?

_____

_____

_____

_____

_____

What did you learn about this sense?

_____

_____

_____

_____

_____

What can you do to remain aware of this sense?

_____

_____

_____

_____

_____

Rate this Sense: ☐ Attraction ☐ Neutral ☐ Aversion

Horticultural sense (the desire and ability to nurture gardens and cultivate crops) (#29)

- ✿ What do you plant, grow, or harvest?
- ✿ What are your favourite plants or trees and why?
- ✿ What plants have you grown in the past that you no longer grow? Why do you not grow them anymore?
- ✿ What do you wish you could grow but can't right now?
- ✿ How does it feel to see plants or seeds you've nurtured thrive? To see them wither and die?
- ✿ Do you have houseplants at home and in your workplace?
  - o If so, take a moment to examine or remember each one in great detail.
  - o If not, visualise where you might put a few house plants indoors.
- ✺ What will you do to bring more direct nurturing of plants into your life?
- ✺ Visit www.TheLandInstitute.org and read about development of perennial crops.

In 1993, Henry David Thoreau's last manuscript, *Faith in a Seed: The Dispersion of Seeds,* was first published. It draws on Charles Darwin's theory of natural selection and refutes the then widely accepted theory that some plants spring spontaneously to life, independent of roots, cuttings, or seeds. He wrote, "I have great faith in a seed. Convince me that you have a seed there, and I am prepared to expect wonders."

Mental Senses

What physical sensations did you experience?

_____

_____

_____

_____

_____

What emotions arose as you explored this sense?

_____

_____

_____

_____

_____

What did you learn about this sense?

_____

_____

_____

_____

_____

What can you do to remain aware of this sense?

_____

_____

_____

_____

_____

Rate this Sense: ☐ Attraction   ☐ Neutral   ☐ Aversion

Sense of mind and consciousness (#30)

- Do the following activities with your eyes closed.
    - Notice all the thoughts you're having.
    - Notice when a thought starts and ends.
    - Is there a space between your thoughts?
    - Have a thought that you'd like to move your right arm – then actually move it.
    - Have a thought to move your arm then decide whether you'll do so.
    - Notice the variety and frequency of your thoughts and the ability you have to direct your thoughts.
- Remember a time that you changed your mind about an important thought.
- Reflect on:
    - How do your thoughts arise?
    - Are you your thoughts?

While consciousness is often attributed to humans following René Descartes notion "I think, therefore I am," there are new studies about animal consciousness, specifically the 2012 Cambridge Declaration on Consciousness. It states that many non-human animals, including mammals and birds, exhibit intentional behaviours such as decision-making, self-recognition, and empathy.

What physical sensations did you experience?

_____

_____

_____

_____

_____

What emotions arose as you explored this sense?

_____

_____

_____

_____

_____

What did you learn about this sense?

_____

_____

_____

_____

_____

What can you do to remain aware of this sense?

_____

_____

_____

_____

_____

Rate this Sense: ☐ Attraction ☐ Neutral ☐ Aversion

Sense of language and articulation, used to express feelings and convey information (#31)

- Remember a poem, song, novel, or lyrics that moved you.
- Remember a time when you were in a situation where you needed to choose your words carefully.
- Have you ever said something that you immediately regretted?
- What words would you use to describe the nature that is around you to someone who is not there?
- Engage in conversations with family, friends, or colleagues and practice active listening by hearing their complete message – not just their words.
    - Pay attention to their words in context of their tone of voice and body language.
    - Observe your own thoughts and how they may be affecting your ability to hear the true message.
    - What can these interactions teach you about your own communication skills and how they might be affecting your relationships?

> Honey bee workers perform the "waggle dance," to indicate the location of food sources. Scout bees fly in search of supplies of pollen and nectar; they return to the hive and "dance" on the honeycomb by walking while shaking their abdomen and buzzing with the beat of their wings. The distance and speed of this movement communicates the distance of the foraging site. The dancing bee aligns her body in the direction of the food, relative to the position of the sun.

What physical sensations did you experience?

_____

_____

_____

_____

_____

What emotions arose as you explored this sense?

_____

_____

_____

_____

_____

What did you learn about this sense?

_____

_____

_____

_____

_____

What can you do to remain aware of this sense?

_____

_____

_____

_____

_____

Rate this Sense: ☐ Attraction   ☐ Neutral   ☐ Aversion

Sense of reason, memory, and capacity for logic and science (#32)

- Reflect on the most complex mental or intellectual activity you have ever done.
    - What physical parts of your body were activated and engaged at that time?
    - Remember your thought processes as you worked through the problem.
- Remember a time when you had an important decision to make.
    - What steps did you take before you chose your final action?
    - What might you do differently if you could do it again?
- Remember a time when you took something apart to figure out how it worked.
- Close your eyes and remember your entire life chronologically, beginning with your earliest memory.

The tiny Honey Guide bird leads Ratels (honey badgers) to beehives. When the bird finds a badger, she flies close to it and chirps while fanning her tail to display her white feathers. When the Ratel notices, he grunts and growls while following her. The bird hops from tree to tree till she is close to the hive and waits for the badger to find it too. After the badger eats the honey, the bird eats the bee larvae and the beeswax.

What physical sensations did you experience?

_____

_____

_____

_____

_____

What emotions arose as you explored this sense?

_____

_____

_____

_____

_____

What did you learn about this sense?

_____

_____

_____

_____

_____

What can you do to remain aware of this sense?

_____

_____

_____

_____

_____

Rate this Sense: ☐ Attraction ☐ Neutral ☐ Aversion

Sense of form, design, and function (#33)

✿ Look at an object in nature and examine its form and design in great detail. What is its function?

✿ Look at a man-made object and do the same.

    o Compare and contrast natural vs. man-made objects.

    o Think about the purpose of each detail in the shape and function of the objects.

    o What emotions arise when you look at a shape from nature vs. a man-made one?

    o How does one feel compared to the other?

�֍ Pay attention to objects you encounter today and do the same analysis.

✖ Notice if there are any objects in your home or office that make you uncomfortable due to the shape, design, or function.

Biomimicry is an approach to innovation that seeks sustainable solutions to human challenges by emulating nature. Materials researchers and engineers at Kansai University in Japan saw amazing potential in the structure of the mosquito's mouth. Scientists used sophisticated engineering techniques that can carve out structures on the nanometer scale. The result of this blend of materials science and biology was a needle that penetrates like a mosquito, using pressure to stabilize and painlessly glide into skin.

What physical sensations did you experience?

_____

_____

_____

_____

_____

What emotions arose as you explored this sense?

_____

_____

_____

_____

_____

What did you learn about this sense?

_____

_____

_____

_____

_____

What can you do to remain aware of this sense?

_____

_____

_____

_____

_____

Rate this Sense: ☐ Attraction ☐ Neutral ☐ Aversion

Sense of play, sport, humour, pleasure, and laughter (#34)

- Remember back through your childhood to how you played and with whom. Compare that to your sense of play today.
- What is the funniest thing you can think of?
- When do you remember laughing till tears came?
- When was the last time you did something really goofy?
- Close your eyes and notice sensations in your body right now. Notice your breathing as you remember the most pleasurable physical sensations you've experienced. Then remember:
    o Being hugged and kissed
    o Receiving a shoulder and neck massage
    o Taking a hot shower or bath
- How can you bring more play, sport, humour, pleasure, and laughter into your life?

Even animals play! Dogs use a posture called "play bow" to invite others to play – their front end is low and their bottom is wiggling in the air. An open mouth and relaxed face are other clues that point to a playful mood. Surprisingly, crocodiles, alligators, and other reptiles also play. More than 15 separate observations have been documented, including playing with bright flowers by carrying them around in their teeth, and by giving their smaller companions piggyback rides.

What physical sensations did you experience?

_____

_____

_____

_____

_____

What emotions arose as you explored this sense?

_____

_____

_____

_____

_____

What did you learn about this sense?

_____

_____

_____

_____

_____

What can you do to remain aware of this sense?

_____

_____

_____

_____

_____

Rate this Sense: ☐ Attraction ☐ Neutral ☐ Aversion

Sense of physical place, navigation senses, awareness of land and seascapes, and of the positions of the sun, moon, and stars (#35)

- Go for a walk around the building you are in.
  - Pay attention to the physical aspects of the building itself.
  - Picture where you are on a street map, a highway map, or a globe
  - Turn your head so you are facing north. How did you know that?
- Remember a place you've been where you are very, very familiar with the layout of the landscape.
  - Close your eyes and imagine walking around this area.
  - How does it make you feel to remember being in that place?
- Remember a time when you were lost and notice any emotions associated with that event. How did you find your way back?
- For one full week, try to notice the position of the sun, moon & stars at different times of the day.

> To memorize the location of their hive, honeybees fly a short way out of the hive, turn around to face the hive entrance, then hover back and forth in ever increasing circles and arcs around and above the hive. These "orientation flights" are how young bees start off, and how all bees re-orient themselves after their hive is moved.

What physical sensations did you experience?

_____

_____

_____

_____

_____

What emotions arose as you explored this sense?

_____

_____

_____

_____

_____

What did you learn about this sense?

_____

_____

_____

_____

_____

What can you do to remain aware of this sense?

_____

_____

_____

_____

_____

Rate this Sense: ☐ Attraction ☐ Neutral ☐ Aversion

Sense of time and rhythm (#36)

⊛ Go outside or look out a window. Notice each living thing and ask yourself:

    o Is it in its prime, past its prime, or has "its time" not yet come?

    o Can you guess the age of each object?

⊛ Remember an event that felt like it just took a moment but actually lasted a long time.

⊛ Remember an event that felt as if it would never end.

⊛ Using your hands or feet,

    o Strike a rhythm with or on your body.

    o Alter the rhythm and compare/contrast how different tempos and patterns feel in your body.

⊛ Close your eyes and notice how you feel as you remember the rhythms of a waltz, heavy metal music, cool jazz, rap music, salsa.

⊛ What rhythms are in nature and how do they relate to the flow of time?

Lightning bugs, also known as fireflies, are beetles that live on the edges of streams and ponds. Males flash their lights to attract females. There are about 136 different species of firefly and each species has its own specific flash pattern that varies by number, duration, and time between flashes. They are the only known insects that flash their lights to give off signals.

What physical sensations did you experience?

_____

_____

_____

_____

_____

What emotions arose as you explored this sense?

_____

_____

_____

_____

_____

What did you learn about this sense?

_____

_____

_____

_____

_____

What can you do to remain aware of this sense?

_____

_____

_____

_____

_____

Rate this Sense: ☐ Attraction ☐ Neutral ☐ Aversion

Sense of biological and astral time (i.e. movement of the stars), awareness of past, present, and future events (#37)

- ❀ Stand in front of a mirror and take a compassionate, non-judgmental close look at your physical body.
    - o Remember how it looked at different stages of your life.
    - o Imagine how it will look in the future.
- ❀ Take a couple of deep breaths and articulate what the phrase "the past" means to you.
    - o Do the same for "the present" and "the future".
    - o What about "ancient past" and "far distant future"?
- ❀ Visualise movement of the planets and stars.
- ❀ Watch https://youtu.be/1wMhBoRfdXA for a time lapse video of the blooming of a ghost orchid.
- ❀ How would you describe what is happening in this moment?
- ✂ At various times during the day, think about what just passed, what is happening in the present, and what might happen in the future.

Mirabilis jalapa flowers, native to Peru, usually open from late afternoon onwards, hence its common name, four o'clock flower. Multi-colored tubular flowers produce a strong, sweet-smelling fragrance throughout the night, then close for good in the morning.

Time and space are modes by which we think, not conditions in which we live.

~ Albert Einstein

What physical sensations did you experience?

_____

_____

_____

_____

_____

What emotions arose as you explored this sense?

_____

_____

_____

_____

What did you learn about this sense?

_____

_____

_____

_____

What can you do to remain aware of this sense?

_____

_____

_____

_____

_____

Rate this Sense: ☐ Attraction ☐ Neutral ☐ Aversion

Sense of meanings, moods and emotions attached to colours, textures, and sounds (#38)

- Look at the variety of colours inside your home.
  - How does each colour make you feel physically?
  - What in nature has these same colours?
  - Do you notice an emotion or mood attached to each colour?
  - How would it feel if your body was each of these colours?
  - Go outside and notice the variety of colours in nature and ask yourself the same questions as above.
  - How do the fabricated colours compare emotionally to colours in nature?
  - Repeat these same questions noticing textures and then sounds.
- What steps can you take to bring more uplifting colours, textures, and sounds into your life?

> Design industry experts forecast annual "colors of the year." International workshops are held where participants share their color insights and stories and discuss big picture trends and influences that will impact color choices over the next two years based on the economy, the environment, politics, sports, social issues, technology, cultural events, and global affairs.

What physical sensations did you experience?

_____

_____

_____

_____

_____

What emotions arose as you explored this sense?

_____

_____

_____

_____

_____

What did you learn about this sense?

_____

_____

_____

_____

_____

What can you do to remain aware of this sense?

_____

_____

_____

_____

_____

Rate this Sense: ☐ Attraction ☐ Neutral ☐ Aversion

Sense of excessive stress and surrender (#39)

- Remember a time when you were extremely stressed and you went to nature for comfort.
  - Where did you go and why?
- Bring to mind one topic that you are stressed or worried about right now.
  - Visualise all the thoughts you have about this topic.
  - Notice any changes in your breathing or muscle tension as you focus your thoughts on this topic.
  - Then, for the next few minutes, centre your attention on a plant or tree near you and notice any change in your breathing or muscle tension as you focus on the plant.
- Remember a time when you were extremely stressed or anxious and you surrendered to it.
  - Why did you surrender and how did it feel?
  - Were there any long-term effects of giving in when you did?
  - Did you fight back before you gave in?
  - Would you do it differently if you had the chance?

Color change is one indication of stress in succulent plants. Most color changes in succulents are a normal response to either excessive cold, heat, sun, nutrient deficiency, or drought. Some plants are purposefully stressed for nursery sales because of the brilliant and ornamental appearances they take on under these situations.

Communal Senses

What physical sensations did you experience?

_____

_____

_____

_____

_____

What emotions arose as you explored this sense?

_____

_____

_____

_____

_____

What did you learn about this sense?

_____

_____

_____

_____

_____

What can you do to remain aware of this sense?

_____

_____

_____

_____

_____

Rate this Sense: ☐ Attraction ☐ Neutral ☐ Aversion

Sense of emotional place, of community, belonging, support, trust, and thankfulness (#40)

⊛ Reflect on the most important relationships in your work as well as your personal life.

   o How would you rate these relationships?

   o What are you most thankful for about these relationships?

   o What could you do today to improve the quality of these relationships?

⊛ Make a list of all groups to which you belong.

   o Review each one and rate the level of belonging, support, trust, and thankfulness you feel when you are with each group.

   o How does it feel emotionally when you are in the company of each group?

   o Which groups feel healthy and empowering? Which do not?

Monarch butterflies migrate up to 2,000 miles to their wintering sites in southern California and northern Mexico. Tens of thousands of them form clusters on the branches of fir trees as they huddle together to survive winter nights and for protection from wind, snow, rain, and hail.

What physical sensations did you experience?

_____

_____

_____

_____

_____

What emotions arose as you explored this sense?

_____

_____

_____

_____

_____

What did you learn about this sense?

_____

_____

_____

_____

What can you do to remain aware of this sense?

_____

_____

_____

_____

Rate this Sense: ☐ Attraction ☐ Neutral ☐ Aversion

Urge to procreate (includes sex awareness, courting, love, mating, and raising young) (#41)

- Reflect back through your lifetime and recall:
    - memories of your first love,
    - emotional sensations of your first kiss,
    - first awareness of your sensual body,
    - sensations of dancing with someone you love,
    - physical sensations from the first time you made love.
- Picture your sense of giving birth or nurturing others and notice how that feels.
- Who or what have you nurtured and/or raised?
- Remember times in your life when you were the caregiver or were responsible for another living being.
- Do you have a sense that you want to leave a legacy or tangible memory of yourself for others?
    - If so, how would you describe the legacy?
    - If not, why not?

Elephant calves are born after a 22-month long pregnancy followed by delivery of the world's largest babies (220 - 250 pounds). Baby elephants are born blind and completely dependent on their mother and a group of young, nurturing female elephants, called "allmothers", who are learning how to rear babies.

117

What physical sensations did you experience?

_____

_____

_____

_____

_____

What emotions arose as you explored this sense?

_____

_____

_____

_____

_____

What did you learn about this sense?

_____

_____

_____

_____

_____

What can you do to remain aware of this sense?

_____

_____

_____

_____

_____

Rate this Sense: ☐ Attraction   ☐ Neutral   ☐ Aversion

Territorial sense (includes possession and ownership; sense of home) (#42)

- Visualise different settings where you have a sense of "your territory."
  - What would make you feel threatened there?
  - Have you ever had to protect your territory?
  - How does it feel to "be in your own territory?"
  - What sensations do you notice when a stranger enters your territory?
- What are your possessions?
  - What have you purchased or acquired and what has been given to you?
  - What possessions could you live without?
  - Which would you fight to keep?
  - Would you kill to protect your possessions?
- Describe your home and contemplate why it feels like "home".
  - Who else is part of your sense of home?
  - Think about each place you have called home; remember who was with you there.

Gray wolves are equally at home in the deserts of Israel, the forests of Wisconsin, and the arctic of Siberia. They were found in most habitats; prairie, forest, mountains, and wetlands. Their territories are typically 50 sq. mi. but may extend up to 1,000 sq. mi. when prey is scarce. Wolves can travel as far as 30 miles a day to hunt.

119

What physical sensations did you experience?

_____

_____

_____

_____

_____

What emotions arose as you explored this sense?

_____

_____

_____

_____

_____

What did you learn about this sense?

_____

_____

_____

_____

_____

What can you do to remain aware of this sense?

_____

_____

_____

_____

_____

Rate this Sense: ☐ Attraction ☐ Neutral ☐ Aversion

Sense of awareness of one's own visibility or invisibility and the ability to camouflage (#43)

- Sit or stand outside where you are sheltered by a tree, shrub or wall.
    - o Situate yourself so you can see out but it would be difficult for others to see you.
    - o What makes you feel invisible in this setting?
    - o What is the sensation in your physical body when you are hidden? How does it feel emotionally?
- Remember a time when you were in a group setting and you faded into the background. What did you do to make yourself feel that way?
- Remember a time when you were the centre of attention and felt that you were in full view. What did you do to make yourself feel that way?
- In general, do you tend to make yourself visible or invisible? Why? Which makes you feel more comfortable?
- Experiment with this sense in different settings and with different groups of people.

Some animals will incorporate bits of their environment onto their bodies for camouflage. Three-toed sloths have algae growing in their fur, which gives them a dark green hue that helps them hide among the trees. Coral crabs attach young polyps to their shells so they resemble part of the reef.

What physical sensations did you experience?

_____

_____

_____

_____

_____

What emotions arose as you explored this sense?

_____

_____

_____

_____

_____

What did you learn about this sense?

_____

_____

_____

_____

_____

What can you do to remain aware of this sense?

_____

_____

_____

_____

_____

Rate this Sense: ☐ Attraction ☐ Neutral ☐ Aversion

Awareness of the capacity to persuade, mesmerize, or hypnotize other creatures (#44)

- ✿ Think about a situation when you were at your most persuasive.
    - o What were you doing?
    - o How did you feel?
    - o How did it make others feel?
    - o What were the results?
- ✿ Did you ever want to be persuasive but failed?
- ✿ Remember a time when you were mesmerized or transfixed by someone else.
    - o How did you feel physically, emotionally, or intellectually during and after that time?
- ✿ When have you been spellbound by listening to music, reading a book, or attending a play or movie?
    - o What was it that kept your attention so focused?
    - o What physical sensations did you notice when you came back to your normal state of awareness?

More than 300 species of spiders are known to mimic the outward appearance of ants, a phenomenon called myrmecomorphy. These spiders have a "false waist" to simulate the three-segmented bodies of ants. The spiders behave like ants by waving their front pair of legs near their heads like antennae, and adopting an erratic zig-zag pattern of movement that is more like ants than spiders. These spiders, pretending to be harmless ants, feast on the eggs and young of other spiders.

What physical sensations did you experience?

_____

_____

_____

_____

_____

What emotions arose as you explored this sense?

_____

_____

_____

_____

_____

What did you learn about this sense?

_____

_____

_____

_____

_____

What can you do to remain aware of this sense?

_____

_____

_____

_____

_____

Rate this Sense: ☐ Attraction ☐ Neutral ☐ Aversion

Sense of self (includes power, control, dominance, and submission) (#45)

⚘ What words would you use to introduce yourself to a new acquaintance?

⚘ Describe yourself as if someone was going to write your biography.

⚘ Remember a time when you were in power or in a position of dominance and had complete control over others. How did this feel?

⚘ Do you remember a situation when you were in complete submission or felt powerless with the situation or group or person?

  o Why were you powerless?

  o Would you respond in the same way if you were in the same situation again?

⚘ Do you change your body language, tone of voice, or personality when you are with certain people or groups? Why or why not?

⚘ Explore your sense of power in various aspects of your life – at work, in relationships, with pets, etc. Rate your strengths and weaknesses.

Wolf packs have an elaborate hierarchy. Alpha males (or Alpha pairs) eat first, make most of the decisions, and are usually the only ones to mate and produce offspring. Packs also include Beta males, Subordinates, and Juvenile wolves, as well as Omega wolves - the weakest or least skilled who feed last or not at all.

What physical sensations did you experience?

_____

_____

_____

_____

_____

What emotions arose as you explored this sense?

_____

_____

_____

_____

_____

What did you learn about this sense?

_____

_____

_____

_____

_____

What can you do to remain aware of this sense?

_____

_____

_____

_____

_____

Rate this Sense: ☐ Attraction   ☐ Neutral   ☐ Aversion

Urge to travel, migrate, emigrate, and colonize (including compassion and receptive awareness of all the earth's living beings) (#46)

⚘ When have you experienced an urge to travel or emigrate? How did it feel?

⚘ Many animals migrate back to the site of their birth to lay eggs or raise their young (Canada Goose, Loggerhead Sea Turtles.) Have you ever gone back to your childhood home? Why or why not?

⚘ Many plants and trees form colonies when they find a location that suits their needs. Do you know of human groups who have done the same?

⚘ Human migration and refugee flight are commonplace around the globe.

- o Why do people do this?
- o Why are some refugees welcomed while others are shunned or turned away?
- o What is the life of a refugee like in a new setting where they don't know the language?

Cranes, swans, and geese learn to migrate by following their parents. When the last bird to use the route dies, so does that knowledge. In 2001, Whooping Crane Eastern Partnership led 7 captive-raised, endangered Whooping Cranes from Wisconsin to Florida using ultralight planes to imprint the route. 6 of the 7 returned to Wisconsin, on their own, the next spring.

What physical sensations did you experience?

_____

_____

_____

_____

_____

What emotions arose as you explored this sense?

_____

_____

_____

_____

_____

What did you learn about this sense?

_____

_____

_____

_____

_____

What can you do to remain aware of this sense?

_____

_____

_____

_____

_____

Rate this Sense: ☐ Attraction ☐ Neutral ☐ Aversion

Sense of survival through joining a more established organism (#47)

- Remember a time you felt that you needed support from others.
    - o Did you seek out help or not?
    - o If you did, how did it feel before and then after you reached out for help?
    - o If you did not, why not? If you could do it over, would you reach out?
- What communities are you a part of now?
    - o How does each support you?
    - o How does it feel when you are in the presence of members of these communities?
    - o How does each community support your sense of survival?
- Do you have a memory of doing something just to survive?
- Is there some aspect to your life now that would benefit from being in a supportive or more established community? What will you do to find one?

Emperor penguins huddle together during snow storms. Normally penguins are very territorial and will not approach each other easily, but this behaviour is one of the ways that emperor penguins survive successfully in the Antarctic winter. There is a constant changing of position from the outside to the inside and during a snow storm lasting days, the whole huddle will slowly move a couple of hundred meters or more.

Spiritual Senses

What physical sensations did you experience?

_____

_____

_____

_____

_____

What emotions arose as you explored this sense?

_____

_____

_____

_____

_____

What did you learn about this sense?

_____

_____

_____

_____

_____

What can you do to remain aware of this sense?

_____

_____

_____

_____

_____

Rate this Sense: ☐ Attraction ☐ Neutral ☐ Aversion

Aesthetic sense (includes creativity and appreciation of beauty, music, literature, form, design, and drama) (#48)

⊛ Make a list of those things you consider to be absolutely beautiful.

⊛ Spend a few moments on each of these questions:

- o What music makes you feel uplifted and joyful? What music does the opposite?
- o What literature expands your thoughts and intellect?
- o What is the most glorious piece of art in the world?
- o What are the most enticing places in nature?
- o What is the best play or movie you've attended?

⊛ What objects in your home and office express your personal sense of aesthetics?

⊛ What is your personal talent for expressing beauty, music, literature, etc.?

- o What are you doing in your life right now to share this gift?
- o What are your creative outlets?

Salish artist Jaune Quick-to-See-Smith writes, "Each tribe's total culture is immersed in its specific area. Traditional foods, ceremonies, and art come from the indigenous plants and animals as well as the land itself. The anthropomorphism of the land spawns the stories and myths. These things are the stuff of culture which keep identity intact."

What physical sensations did you experience?

_____

_____

_____

_____

_____

What emotions arose as you explored this sense?

_____

_____

_____

_____

_____

What did you learn about this sense?

_____

_____

_____

_____

_____

What can you do to remain aware of this sense?

_____

_____

_____

_____

_____

Rate this Sense: ☐ Attraction ☐ Neutral ☐ Aversion

Sense of humility, ethics, morality, and fairness (#49)

- Remember a time you accomplished something that was difficult or complex.
    - Did you have a sense of pride?
    - How did it feel to receive praise from others?
- Have you ever felt humbled by something you accomplished?
- Think of a situation when something just didn't seem fair. Why not?
- Define your personal sense of ethics, morality and fairness.
    - Remember a time you acted ethically even if it was not supported by others.
    - Remember a time you did not act ethically because of someone else's opinion or actions.
    - What is your reaction when others you are with do not act ethically?
    - Is there an aspect of your life right now that just doesn't feel right?
- What might you do to live a more ethical life?

> Researchers at the University of Chicago found that when one rat was placed near another jailed rat, the free rat would open the hatch for a rescue — something it wouldn't do for a toy rat. What's more, when given the choice between saving a fellow rat and eating some chocolate, the free rat would open both cells and then share.

What physical sensations did you experience?

_____

_____

_____

_____

_____

What emotions arose as you explored this sense?

_____

_____

_____

_____

_____

What did you learn about this sense?

_____

_____

_____

_____

_____

What can you do to remain aware of this sense?

_____

_____

_____

_____

_____

Rate this Sense: ☐ Attraction ☐ Neutral ☐ Aversion

Intuition or subconscious deduction sense (a.k.a. sixth sense) (#50)

⊛ Describe your understanding of the word "intuition."

⊛ Remember a time when you acted on your intuition, a gut feeling, or instinct.

    o Were there any physical sensations in your body that helped you make a decision about this feeling?

    o What thoughts did you have as you decided to act on this intuition?

⊛ Remember when you had an intuition but chose not to act on it.

    o Why did you make this choice?

⊛ Were you taught to trust or distrust your intuitions?

⊛ Have you ever had a sense that you just "knew" something even though you had never studied it?

⊛ Did you ever have a sense of déjà vu, the feeling that you have already experienced something that is actually happening for the first time?

More research studies have been done on intuition's role for nurses than in any other healthcare profession, based on this definition, "Intuition is the sudden perception of a pattern in a seemingly unrelated series of events.... Beyond what is visible to the senses." Because of the positive research on intuition in nursing, teams at Abbott NW Hospital in Minnesota receive intuition training and integrate it into their daily activities.

137

What physical sensations did you experience?

_____

_____

_____

_____

_____

What emotions arose as you explored this sense?

_____

_____

_____

_____

_____

What did you learn about this sense?

_____

_____

_____

_____

What can you do to remain aware of this sense?

_____

_____

_____

_____

_____

Rate this Sense: ☐ Attraction ☐ Neutral ☐ Aversion

Sense of relaxation and sleep (includes dreaming, meditation, and brain wave awareness) (#51)

- Close your eyes & notice your level of brain activity right now – rate it from 1(low) -10 (high).
    - Set an alarm for 5 minutes then watch your breath and count how long it takes for each exhalation and inhalation until the alarm goes off.
    - Rate your level of brain activity at the end of 5 minutes.
- Remember a time when you were on high alert or fearful; what was your level of brain activity?
- Let your mind wander back to a dream you remember. Try to re-create the dream in your imagination and notice your level of brain activity.
- What does it mean to be completely relaxed and how does that differ from sleep or meditation?
- Pay attention to your brain activity and rate it when you just start to drift off to sleep, when you first wake up in the morning, and while you're at work, in meditation, and during exercise.

Many of the great wisdom traditions teach "dream yoga." Before you go to sleep, hold the clear intention to wake up and be conscious within your dreams. In some Native American traditions, dreamers are advised to look at their hands within a dream, or to raise their hands to the sky in a prayer for rain to bless the earth. Learning to wake up within our dreams, and see and understand deeply and clearly what is going on, can be a profound path of awakening.

What physical sensations did you experience?

_____

_____

_____

_____

_____

What emotions arose as you explored this sense?

_____

_____

_____

_____

_____

What did you learn about this sense?

_____

_____

_____

_____

_____

What can you do to remain aware of this sense?

_____

_____

_____

_____

_____

Rate this Sense: ☐ Attraction ☐ Neutral ☐ Aversion

Psychic sense (includes foreknowledge, clairvoyance, clairaudience, psychokinesis, telepathy, astral projection, and certain animal instincts and plant sensitivities) (#52)

- Remember a coincidence or synchronistic event that had a powerful impact on you.
- Have you ever had a dream that came true?
- Cutting edge research is starting to show that plants have their own consciousness and are able to communicate with us. Keep an open mind and try this exercise:
  - o Bring your awareness to your favourite plant or tree.
  - o Spend a few minutes using all your senses to notice every detail about it while you stroke its leaves or touch its bark.
  - o When you feel relaxed, ask the plant a question, as if you could have a conversation with it.
  - o Listen for an answer in your body via a thought, feeling or sensation. Don't judge it or analyse it; notice whatever comes to mind.
- Do you have any of the psychic senses listed above?
  - o Do you know someone who does?
  - o What are your thoughts about these abilities?

> Animal totems come from the Native American culture. Totems are animal spirit guides who serve as messengers to help us gain insights, self-awareness, enhance our connection to the past, and even see glimpses of future events.

What physical sensations did you experience?

_____

_____

_____

_____

_____

What emotions arose as you explored this sense?

_____

_____

_____

_____

_____

What did you learn about this sense?

_____

_____

_____

_____

_____

What can you do to remain aware of this sense?

_____

_____

_____

_____

_____

Rate this Sense: ☐ Attraction ☐ Neutral ☐ Aversion

Spiritual sense (includes conscience, capacity for divine/universal love, ecstasy, deep joy, profound sorrow, sacrifice, and compassion) (#53)

❀ Remember a time you took a certain action because your conscience told you to. How did it feel?

❀ Were you ever in a situation when you did NOT follow your conscience? How did it feel?

❀ What have you sacrificed in your life? Why? Would you do it again?

❀ Visualise a moment when you experienced profound joy. What happens to your breath as you remember?

❀ Remember a time of profound sorrow. Was there a spiritual aspect to this sense of grief?

❀ When have you experienced a sense of deep empathetic compassion?

❀ Do you believe there is a higher power over all life?

   o If yes, how has your perception of an awareness of a spiritual aspect to life changed throughout your lifetime?

   o If no, how would you describe your own beliefs about all that you experience in life?

❀ Sublime love is an expression of awe and reverence. What gives you a feeling of awe and reverence?

A graceful shorebird, the Killdeer demonstrates the concept of sacrifice in two ways. It puts on a broken-wing act to lead predators away from its nest, and to protect its eggs from being stepped on by cows it fluffs itself up, displays its tail over its head, and runs at the beast to attempt to make it change its path.

What physical sensations did you experience?

_____

_____

_____

_____

_____

What emotions arose as you explored this sense?

_____

_____

_____

_____

_____

What did you learn about this sense?

_____

_____

_____

_____

_____

What can you do to remain aware of this sense?

_____

_____

_____

_____

_____

Rate this Sense: ☐ Attraction ☐ Neutral ☐ Aversion

Sense of interconnectedness/oneness/unity (#54)

⊛ Reflect on your understanding of the word "interconnectedness" in light of this quote from naturalist John Muir, *"When we try to pick out anything by itself, we find it hitched to everything else in the Universe."*

- o What do you know about the relationship between sunlight and the food you eat?
- o About insects and fruit production?
- o What are you connected to and what connects to you?

⊛ Imagine that you could explore these 54 Senses through the eyes and experiences of others.

- o How would that affect your thoughts about how others act?
- o How would that alter your sense of oneness?

⊛ Re-read through the list of the first 53 Senses.

- o Savour each one individually then perceive them as a whole picture of who you are.
- o How does it feel to recognise within yourself the same senses that define all living beings?
- o Is there a sense of unity, completeness, or wholeness about your relationship to humanity as well as to the natural world?

> Mitakuye Oyasin (all things are connected) are words of wise insight from the Lakota Sioux nation that knows the importance of living in harmony with nature. The Native American prayer teaches the oneness of all forms of life: people, animals, birds, insects, trees and plants, and even rocks, rivers, mountains.

145

What's Next?

⚛ If you haven't already done so, follow this link to listen to "Re-Activate Your 54 Senses" by Tabitha Jayne: www.thenatureprocess.co/54sensesmeditation

⚛ Start back at the beginning of this workbook and go through all the 54 Senses again – perhaps in a different order or different setting.

⚛ Revisit the senses you marked as "Neutral" or "Aversion" and see if you have a different reaction. Explore these senses in different settings or at various times of day.

⚛ Draw, paint, or sculpt some of your experiences with different senses.

⚛ Gather a group of friends to explore this workbook together in a favourite place in nature or meet weekly over a year's time to delve deeply into one sense each week.

⚛ Expand your knowledge of The Nature Process by visiting www.TheNatureProcess.co and see what events, webinars, or books are available.

⚛ Consider deepening and sharing your experience by becoming a facilitator of The Nature Process. See www.TheNatureProcess.co/Training

References and Resources

2012 Cambridge Declaration on Consciousness. 2012. http://fcmconference.org/img/CambridgeDeclarationOnConsciousness.pdf

Benyus, Janine M. *Biomimicry: innovation inspired by nature.* New York, Perennial, 2002. www.biomimicry.org

Buhner, Stephen Harrod. *Plant intelligence and the imaginal realm: beyond the doors of perception into the dreaming earth.* Rochester, VT, Bear & Company, 2014.

Buhner, Stephen Harrod. *The Secret Teachings of Plants; The Intelligence of the Heart in the Direct Perception of Nature.* Rochester, VT, Bear & Company, 2004.

Carson, Rachel, and Charles Pratt. *The sense of wonder.* New York, Harper & Row, 1965.

Chalquist, Craig, and Mary E. Gomes. *Terrapsychology: re-Engaging the soul of place.* New Orleans, Spring Journal Books, 2007.

Clifford, M. Amos. *A Little Handbook of Shinrin-Yoku.* The Association of Nature And Forest Therapy, 2013. www.natureandforesttherapy.org

Cohen, Michael J. "Educating, Counseling and Healing with Nature: Ecopsychology in Action. Applied Ecotherapy." *Ecopsychology in Action,* www.ecopsych.com/.

Conroy, Jim, and Basia Alexander. *Tree whispering: a nature lover's guide to touching, healing, and communicating with trees, plants, and all of nature.* Morris Plains, NJ, Plant Kingdom Communications, 2011.

"Innovation Inspired by Nature." *AskNature,* asknature.org/.

Jayne, Tabitha. *The Nature Process (2ⁿᵈ Edition): Deepen Your Connection to Nature, Boost Your Well-being and Enhance Your Life.* TNP Press, 2017.

Jung, C. G., and Meredith Sabini. *The earth has a soul: C.G. Jung on nature, technology & modern life.* Berkeley, CA, North Atlantic Books, 2008.

Louv, Richard. *Last child in the woods: saving our children from nature-deficit disorder.* Chapel Hill, NC, Algonquin Books of Chapel Hill, 2005.

Muir, John, and Linnie Marsh Wolfe. *John of the mountains: the unpublished journals of John Muir.* Boston, Houghton, Mifflin, 1938.

Murchie, Guy. *The seven mysteries of life: an exploration in science & philosophy.* Boston, Houghton Mifflin, 1978.

"Natural Systems Agriculture." *The Land Institute*, www.landinstitute.org/.

Roszak, Theodore. *The voice of the earth.* New York, Simon & Schuster, 1992.

Sewall, Laura. *Sight and sensibility: the ecopsychology of perception.* New York, J.P. Tarcher/Putnam, 1999.

Thoreau, Henry David, and Bradley P. Dean. *Faith in a seed: the dispersion of seeds, and other late natural history writings.* Washington, D.C., Island Press Shearwater Books, 1993.

"Whooping Crane Eastern Partnership." *Whooping Crane Eastern Partnership*, www.bringbackthecranes.org/.

Pay It Forward

Each sale of this workbook supports the social and economic independence of one child in India by sponsoring horticulture training for eight one-hour sessions in a month.

This project, managed by Bombay Mothers & Children Society, aims to educate the younger generation with improved farming techniques and technology, such as greenhouse technology, which will eventually result in a better yield of crops and farm products, as well as to augment their income.

We make our contribution through our parent company EarthSelf's lifetime partnership with Buy One/Give One (B1G1). B1G1 is a social enterprise and non-profit organization with a mission to create a world that's full of giving. 100% of all contributions made to B1G1 go directly to their projects.

For more information about B1G1 go to: www.B1G1.com.

About Sami Aaron

Following two years of leading workshops, seminars, presentations, and retreats on The Nature Process as a certified facilitator, Sami Aaron became the Director of Training and Development for The Nature Process in November 2016.

Sami co-created The Nature Process Facilitator Training program and is responsible for not only leading the training program, but for guiding and mentoring the certified facilitators to develop new programs within their communities. She also is responsible for developing and maintaining the Continuing Professional Development Program for all certified facilitators.

Sami is a registered yoga and meditation teacher and has spent over a decade teaching others contemplative, breathing, and restorative practices through her specialization in Yoga Nidra (yoga sleep) and Pranayama (yoga breathing). She is also a Level 1 Instructor in Mindful Resilience for Trauma Recovery with the Veterans Yoga Project whose mission is to support recovery and resilience among veterans, active duty military, their families, and our communities.

Through her K-State Extension Master Naturalist certification, Sami offers workshops to homeowners and public groups to teach how to create wildflower gardens and explain how restored native areas prevent flooding, clean toxins from our waters, and reduce the amount of city water we use, while replenishing habitat for declining populations of pollinators and other wildlife. The bonus is that these natural areas also connect us to the stress-reduction benefits that come from time spent in nature via the colours, scents, and sensations of vibrant, native gardens that evolve and change through all seasons.

Additionally, Sami is a member of the Green Business Network Kansas City, a network of environmental professionals and business people who all share a common goal: making sustainable business decisions that protect our natural resources AND make good business sense.

Sami is the author of "The Gift of Compassion" published in *Chicken Soup for the Soul, Grieving and Recovery.*

She can be contacted at Sami@TheNatureProcess.co.

Acknowledgements

I wish, first, to thank my students of The Nature Process who have attended workshops, retreats, weekly series, and private sessions. You have taught me the importance of being in natural presence and how easy it is to access that state through the 54 Senses.

For my friend and first yoga teacher, Patricia Gray, along with all my yoga and meditation teachers, thank you for showing me how to find the stillness.

Deep gratitude to good friends Dena Klein and Linda Garrett for their valuable suggestions on format and content. And to Kelly Daniels for her inspired snippets of Native American concepts and philosophy.

Thanks to my sister, Joli Winer, for opening my eyes to the power of the natural world and for her beekeeping experience and lore.

A special thanks to my husband who is always willing to support me through whatever changes occur in my professional life, even as he muffles his eye-rolling when my ideas are way out beyond his comfort zone.

I am grateful to the depths of my soul to my sons for humouring me on our garden strolls and for teaching me about meals prepared with love and the healing powers of nature.

I know I'll never be able to express the depth of my gratitude to Tabitha Jayne for her inspiration in bringing The Nature Process to light and embracing my insistence that I be actively involved in its growth and development. Deep appreciation goes to Lyn Mann for her patient and nature-driven support in The Nature Process and EarthSelf. I know I've found my earth sisters in you both.

And of course, I send endless gratitude to the colossal oak tree in Olathe, the wildflowers and undulating hills of the tallgrass prairie in the Flint Hills, and the intoxicating aroma of the eucalyptus grove in Oakland - you know who you are - for the profound healing you've gifted to me.

Index

Index of Interesting Facts

Note: This index lists the Sense number(s) where the interesting facts can be found.

Made in the USA
Lexington, KY
20 April 2017